Stories of World War II

EVACUATION
IN WORLD WAR II

By A. J. Stones

WAYLAND

First published in 2014 by Wayland
Copyright © Wayland 2014

Wayland
338 Euston Road
London NW1 3BH

Wayland Australia
Level 17/207 Kent Street
Sydney, NSW 2000

Editor: Elizabeth Brent
Designer: Elaine Wilkinson
Researchers: Hester Vaizey, Ela Kaczmarska and Edward Field at
The National Archives

The National Archives, London, England.
www.nationalarchives.gov.uk

The National Archives looks after the UK government's historical documents. It holds records dating back nearly 1,000 years, from the time of William the Conqueror's Domesday Book to the present day. All sorts of documents are stored there, including letters, photographs, maps and posters. They include records of great Kings and Queens, famous rebels like Guy Fawkes and the strange and unusual – such as reports of UFOs and even a mummified rat!

CONTENTS

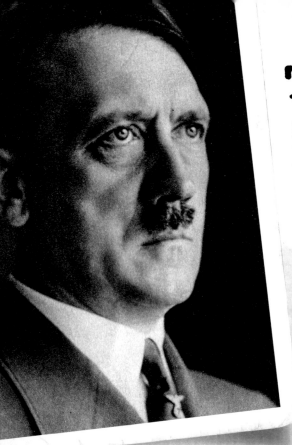

The fear of war

When Adolf Hitler took control of Germany in 1933, the British government was worried that a war would begin. Hitler's Nazi Party wanted to create a new German Empire, and quickly expanded their army. They invaded Austria and Czechoslovakia in 1938, and Poland in 1939. The government was afraid that, in the event of war, German planes would bomb Britain. They needed a plan to keep people safe.

Planning and preparation

The British government decided to protect their civilians by evacuating them to safer areas of the country. Sir John Anderson, a Member of Parliament, formed the Air Raid Precautions (ARP) committee in May 1938, which spent three months planning the evacuation. Relocating hundreds of thousands of civilians was a huge task, so the ARP committee talked to the police, teachers and railway workers to ensure it went smoothly.

LEAVE HITLER TO ME SONNY — **YOU** OUGHT TO BE OUT OF LONDON

ISSUED BY THE MINISTRY OF HEALTH

A newspaper headline announces the beginning of Operation Pied Piper.

Operation Pied Piper

In early 1939, the government began to put together a list of houses that could take evacuees. The scheme was advertised on posters and the radio, and potential hosts were interviewed. The evacuation plan, code-named Operation Pied Piper, was announced on 31st August 1939, and began the next day. Neville Chamberlain, the British Prime Minister, declared war on Germany just two days later, on 3rd September.

Millions moved

In the first two days of the evacuation, 1.5 million people were moved to the countryside. Most of them were school children but other vulnerable people, such as pregnant women, mothers with babies and the disabled, were also evacuated. By the time World War II ended, around 3.5 million people had been moved.

AN UNUSUAL NAME

Operation Pied Piper was named after an old fairy tale, *The Pied Piper of Hamelin*, which tells of a man who steals a village's children using his magic flute to play music and lure them away. Unlike this tale, however, the plan was always to send all the evacuees back home!

Threat from above

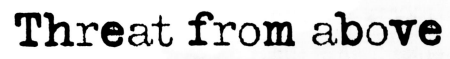

Following the outbreak of war, Germany wanted to invade Britain, so they sent their air force, the Luftwaffe, to attack from the skies. Their aim was to wipe out parts of the country that contained important industries and large residential areas, weakening the British military and destroying the population's morale.

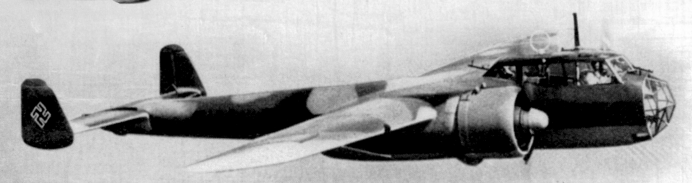

Lightning war

The bombing of Britain began on 7th September 1940. The newspapers quickly called the period between September 1940 and May 1941 'the Blitz', after the German word for 'lightning'. The Luftwaffe targeted industrial cities such as Coventry and Sheffield, hoping to damage factories and warehouses, and reduce the amount of supplies available to the British army. They also attacked large ports, such as Hull, as well as smaller seaside towns like Eastbourne, and old cathedral cities such as Canterbury.

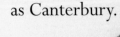

Blackouts

To make it harder for enemy planes to see their targets, blackout regulations were imposed on 1st September 1939. All buildings had to have their windows and doors covered with curtains, cardboard or paint, so no light could escape from inside. All outside lights, including street lamps, were turned off. Any lights that were too important to be turned off completely, such as traffic lights or vehicle headlights, were either dimmed or fitted with covers, so their beams shone straight at the ground.

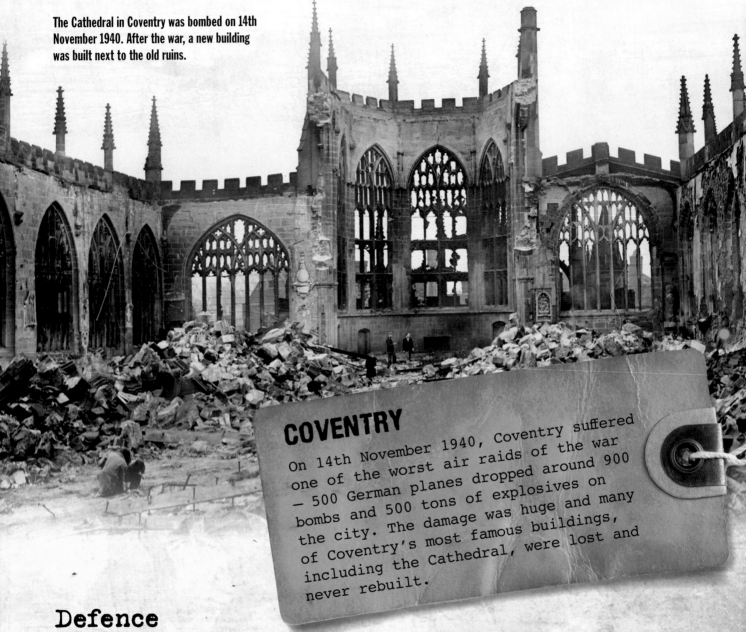

The Cathedral in Coventry was bombed on 14th November 1940. After the war, a new building was built next to the old ruins.

COVENTRY

On 14th November 1940, Coventry suffered one of the worst air raids of the war — 500 German planes dropped around 900 bombs and 500 tons of explosives on the city. The damage was huge and many of Coventry's most famous buildings, including the Cathedral, were lost and never rebuilt.

Defence

The only way to prevent an air raid was to shoot down the Luftwaffe's planes. Anti-aircraft guns were placed on the ground below the planes' expected flight paths. These could be small, rapid-fire machine guns or larger guns capable of sending exploding shells high into the air. RAF fighter planes were also used to combat enemy bombers. Two of the best were the Supermarine Spitfire and the Hawker Hurricane.

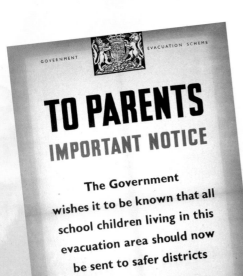

TO PARENTS
IMPORTANT NOTICE

The Government wishes it to be known that all school children living in this evacuation area should now be sent to safer districts

REGISTER AT ONCE AT

Leaving home

Evacuees left from their local train station on specially organised services. Children were often arranged in school groups and they waited on the platform together. Thousands of teachers went with them to ensure they reached the correct destination. They tried to keep brothers and sisters together, but this wasn't always possible.

List of items

Along with their gas mask and identity card, the government recommended that evacuees took the following clothes:

Boys	Girls
2 vests	1 vest
2 pairs of pants	1 pair of pants
1 pair of trousers	1 petticoat
2 pairs of socks	2 pairs of stockings
6 handkerchiefs	6 handkerchiefs
1 pullover or jersey	1 slip
	1 blouse
	1 cardigan
	1 skirt

Their luggage

Evacuees were given a list of items to take with them. It included a change of clothes and food for the journey. Many ignored the advice, however, and wore their smartest clothes. It was also common for evacuees to carry a square cardboard box on a string, which contained their gas mask. Those without suitcases took important items like their pyjamas and toothbrush in a paper bag. Others carried nothing but their favourite teddy bear to keep them company on the journey.

NATIONAL REGISTRATION

IDENTITY

Trouble at the stations

It was difficult to organise the large groups of nervous people at the train stations. As many as one in six children did not turn up, and mothers with babies were often late. This meant that the number of children who were actually evacuated was much lower than expected. Trains couldn't always leave when they planned to, and many evacuees caught the wrong train in the confusion and were taken to the wrong destination.

Parents left behind

A government report from 1st September 1939 claimed that the spirit of the children being evacuated was excellent. Parents were allowed on the platform as their children boarded the carriages, but they tried not to show how worried they were. The children would have had no idea that some of them would be away from home for six years. They may only have realised the seriousness of the situation when they saw their parents crying on the platform.

A group of education and billeting officers at Kingsbridge Station in Devon check their paperwork ready for the arrival of evacuees.

The arms of strangers

If parents had friends or relatives in the countryside, they would ask them to take their children during the war. However, this wasn't an option for many families and their children still needed to leave the city, so they were sent to live with complete strangers.

Choosing a child

When the evacuees arrived at their destination, they lined up to find out who they would be living with. There were not always enough places for everyone, and sometimes the hosts argued over the children they wanted. The smartest dressed were chosen before those who were dirty or sick, and girls were usually picked before boys, because the hosts thought they would be less trouble. As a result, brothers and sisters were sometimes split up and taken to different houses many miles apart.

A group of evacuees from Bristol arrive at Brent station in Devon.

Strange new homes

Evacuees had no idea what their new living arrangements would be like until they arrived at their hosts' houses. Many of them had to share rooms with other children, or even the homeowner. Some hosts were worried about evacuees bringing lice and other skin diseases into their homes, so many were scrubbed and had their heads shaved on arrival. Some evacuees never got used to being away from their parents, and bed-wetting was a common problem. However, others liked their new home better than their old one, particularly the chance to use inside toilets for the first time.

WALLASEY

Wallasey, in Cheshire, was one village that struggled to find a home for all of its evacuees. An official government report claimed that there were only 900 billets, but the village was expected to take nearly 3,000 children. It took a lot of hard work but everyone was given shelter by 9.30pm on the first night. The majority of children had a bed, although some had to make do with straw on the floor.

A new family

All sorts of people took in evacuees, and life varied dramatically from house to house. Children were placed with huge families, single widows, strict Christians and busy farmers, among others. The type of home they were sent to had a huge impact on their daily life. Some children ate well, others lost weight. Some children worked hard, while others played games.

A billeting officer helps a host to fill out a form, whilst the evacuees she has taken in look on.

Welcomed in

All hosts were given instructions by the government. They were told to look after and care for the unaccompanied children as if they were their own. Most people had volunteered their services, and were happy to have another person in the house. Many families had husbands and sons who were away fighting in the war. They treated the evacuees as additional members of the family.

HELP THE CITY CHILDREN

making a new home for Evacuees is a National Service.

ISSUED BY THE MINISTRY OF HEALTH

House rules

Host families received ten shillings and six pence a week (around £15 in today's money) for one child in their care. If they took in more than one child then they received eight shillings and six pence for each (around £12 today). This payment covered the evacuees' board and lodgings, but their hosts had to pay for new clothes and medical expenses themselves.

Made to work

Some hosts did not like having an evacuee in their home, and had been forced to take one. It wasn't unusual for these hosts to use the children as unpaid servants. They gave them chores to do such as tidying up, or polishing the furniture and ornaments. Hosts could be strict, and slap or cane the evacuees if they didn't work hard enough. If the chores took too long, children were late for school and punished further.

An evacuee from France polishes shoes at a hostel for European refugees and British evacuees in Gloucestershire.

FOOD

Evacuees were expected to be fed like any other child. To make sure they ate well, the government sent out a sample menu. Breakfast usually consisted of weak tea and porridge with bread and butter. Dinner was a hot meal such as stewed steak or a hot-pot. Sweet treats like currant rolls or boiled apple pudding were very popular.

Back to school

Evacuees needed to continue their education, but the local schools struggled to find room for them. If the evacuees joined regular lessons, there could be around 70 pupils in one room. Large country houses were used to create temporary classrooms and schools began a 'double-shift' system. Local children were taught in the morning, and the evacuees attended afternoon lessons.

The classroom

Teachers during the war were often elderly, brought out of retirement to replace younger teachers who were serving in the Armed Forces. There was also a shortage of equipment. Pupils had to share pencils, and teachers checked each exercise book to make sure no paper was wasted. Occasionally, young teachers returned from the war on leave and visited the pupils.

Lessons

Education during World War II was sometimes very basic. Children were only taught simple maths, and lessons focused more on singing and studying classic plays. If the weather was good, classes were taken outside, either to play games or to write and read in the sunshine. This made rooms available for other lessons and kept the children active. Children also spent time writing letters to the Royal Navy, and the girls knitted navy blue caps, scarves and sweaters for the sailors. Replies to the letters described the sailors' duties on board their ships.

Class differences

Local children did not always welcome the evacuees. Their schools were suddenly overcrowded with new pupils. The evacuees wore city clothes and spoke with odd accents. It wasn't unusual for the children to get into fights in the playground. To entertain the newcomers, schools often put on shows where the children would sing songs for their parents and hosts. As the evacuees got to know the people around them, they began to feel more comfortable and accepted.

SEPARATED BY GENDER

School life was very different from how it is now. In some schools girls and boys were kept separate, with an iron fence dividing them in the playground. The only joint activity they had was the Christmas play.

Rationing and shortages

During the war, German submarines sank supply ships, preventing vital provisions from reaching the UK. This meant that food and other supplies were in high demand but short supply. To make sure everything was shared out fairly, the government began a system of rationing.

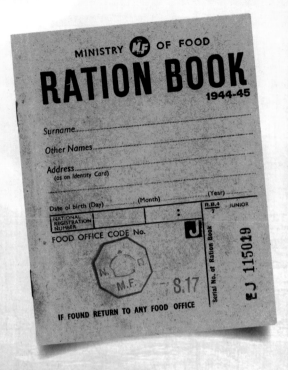

MINISTRY OF FOOD

RATION BOOK
1944-45

Surname.........................

Other Names.........................

Address.........................
(as on Identity Card)

Date of birth (Day) .... (Month) .... (Year) ....

NATIONAL REGISTRATION NUMBER ....

FOOD OFFICE CODE No. ....

R.B.4 JUNIOR
7

Serial No. of Ration Book

EJ 115019

N. M.F. 8.17

IF FOUND RETURN TO ANY FOOD OFFICE

Ration books

Rationing officially began on 8th January 1940. The government issued ration books to everyone – adults received a brown book and children, a blue one. Pregnant women, new mothers and the sick were given a special green book, which granted them extra supplies of nutritious foods such as cod liver oil, milk and orange juice. Everyone could buy a set amount of food and shop assistants marked each book to show when someone had reached their limit.

Queues at the shops

Everyone wanted to be sure of getting enough to eat, so large queues formed outside the shops. Some of the tastiest items, such as butter, cheese, sugar, jam and sweets, were extremely hard to find. People were encouraged to eat fruit and vegetables instead. Alcohol and cigarettes were also in short supply, and the nation's health actually improved during the period of rationing.

Dig for Victory

The government introduced the Dig For Victory campaign, which encouraged families to grow their own food. Allotment numbers rose from 815,000 at the beginning of the war to 1.4 million in 1943. Pigs, chickens and rabbits were reared in the garden until they were ready to eat, and hens were kept for their eggs. Vegetables were grown on any spare patch of land, including tennis courts, railway embankments and school playing fields. By 1940, wasting food was a criminal offence.

Unusual meals

Certain ingredients were hard to come by, so recipes were adapted to use whatever was available. Meatless stews and 'eggless, sugarless, fat-free' cakes appeared on dining tables around the country. Meat was expensive, so beef and lamb were replaced by spam and whale meat. Carrots appeared in everything, from jam to biscuits. Frozen carrots on sticks were even used as a replacement for ice-lollies.

CLOTHING

Food wasn't the only thing in short supply. Clothes became very simple as ships carrying cloth and fabric from abroad were stopped by the German navy. Women even painted gravy browning on their legs as a replacement for silk stockings. The government distributed a pamphlet called *Make Do and Mend* to every household in Britain, offering advice on how to be frugal and reuse old clothing.

Back in the firing line

Thousands of children and new mothers were evacuated in the first few months of the war, but the bombing didn't start immediately. It appeared as if the UK might not come under attack after all, so many parents brought their children back home.

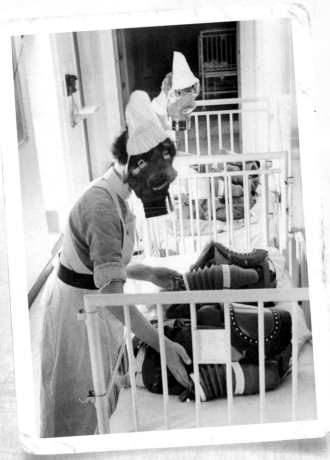

A nurse looks after a baby in a special respirator during a gas drill at a London hospital in 1940.

The Phoney War

The 'Phoney War' is the name given to the eight months after the outbreak of war in September 1939. Until April 1940, there was little evidence of World War II in the UK. In fact, very little military action took place in Western Europe for some time. It seemed as if Neville Chamberlain had declared a war that wasn't really happening.

TAKE THEM BACK!
TAKE THEM BACK!
TAKE THEM BACK!..

DON'T do it, Mother—

LEAVE YOUR CHILDREN IN THE SAFER AREAS

ISSUED BY THE MINISTRY OF HEALTH

Against advice

The government continued to support evacuation, but many parents ignored this advice and brought their children home. The cities were still considered dangerous, but some mothers decided that the countryside was far less safe. The rural towns had no anti-aircraft protection and fewer bomb shelters. Those evacuees with fathers away fighting in the war wanted to be in the city, so they were easier to visit on leave. Many parents were also extremely stressed and unhappy about the enforced separation from their children, and decided to take matters into their own hands. On the whole, evacuees who moved to be with family or friends were more likely to stay than those who were living with strangers.

Kensington

The borough of Kensington in London demonstrates how children moved in and out of the cities. In September 1939, the area housed nearly 10,000 children under the age of five. By October 1939 this had reduced to 4,000. After a few months, nearly 1,000 returned home but when the bombing began, many of the children were re-evacuated.

RUNNING AWAY

If they weren't enjoying their stay, some evacuees left their billets without telling their parents or host families. If they were caught, they were sent back to their host families immediately, so they tried to avoid detection. They were almost always discovered though.

Life in the cities

Everyone living in British cities walked the streets in fear of air raids. Attacks could happen at any time, and with little warning. Sirens alerted the public when planes were approaching and everyone ran for cover.

Air raids

When the largest bombs exploded, they could blow buildings apart with a deafening bang. The blast shattered windows, creating deadly fragments of glass. The explosions started fires, and splinters from bombs could travel over half a mile. After a raid, rescue teams pulled people from the damaged buildings, firefighters put out the flames and ambulances rushed the injured to hospital.

Illness

Air raid shelters forced lots of people to live and sleep within a very small space. The government became concerned about diseases that could be spread this way, including influenza and whooping cough. A *Health in the Shelter* pamphlet was produced to promote the need to keep a shelter clean and tidy. Suggestions included airing the bed and changing your clothes as often as possible.

Running for shelter

The sirens made a wailing sound, which sent everyone into the shelters. Some families had corrugated iron shelters in their garden while others hid in the cupboard under the stairs. There were also public shelters scattered around cities, and schools usually had their own. As the war progressed, many people in London headed underground and onto the tube platforms. On an average night, 60,000 people slept in the tube tunnels, with the government supplying bunk beds and toilets.

Standing strong

People in the shelters kept their spirits up by playing cards, telling jokes and singing songs together. Despite the dangers, children adapted to the change well. School attendance remained good, and doctors' reports remarked that children were 'standing up to the air raids, even better than their parents'.

Space was tight in the underground shelters and children had to make new friends quickly.

GAS MASKS

At the start of the war, people carried gas masks everywhere. Children even had theirs shaped to look like Mickey Mouse. However the Germans never used poison gas, and most people began to leave their masks at home.

Evacuated again

In May 1940, German forces began a large-scale assault on France, Belgium and the Netherlands. Belgium and the Netherlands were conquered within a matter of days and France only lasted a month. Nazi tanks and troops arrived in Paris and France was forced to surrender.

A new danger

France signed an armistice with Germany on 22nd June 1940. The UK's closest ally was now under Nazi control. The threat of invasion increased, so a second evacuation was organised. Between 13th and 18th June 1940, 100,000 children were moved from vulnerable coastal towns in the south and east of England. Some towns in East Anglia and Kent evacuated more than 40% of their population. By July, more than 200,000 children had been relocated, some of them for the second time.

V weapons

In 1944, Britain faced attacks from a new kind of bomb, the 'V weapons'. The first was the V-1, an unmanned 'flying bomb', nicknamed the 'doodlebug' because of the rasping noise it made. When it reached its target, its engine cut out and the bomb fell in silence. The V-2 was even more deadly. It flew so fast that no-one could see or hear it coming. London was the main target for these attacks and they were so hard to stop that children in the city were forced to re-evacuate.

A group of British children arrive in Wellington, New Zealand in 1940.

Going abroad

Official evacuations didn't just send people to safer parts of the UK. Millions of people were moved to other parts of the British Empire including North America, Australia, South Africa and the Caribbean. These countries were harder to get to, but were untouched by the war. Another 2 million wealthy families chose to fund their own evacuation.

OTHER EVACUATIONS

Entire organisations were also evacuated. Under 'Plan Yellow', important government departments were moved to hotels on the west coast or in the centre of quiet Midland towns. Hospitals were also evacuated, to save the lives of their patients. The beds left empty were soon filled with wounded British soldiers who had been rescued from the fighting in France.

Life in the country

During the second evacuation, more areas of the country were at risk. Some children who had been evacuated to the east of England were moved for a second time, and sent to the most remote parts of the country. Suddenly children who were used to city or town life had the chance to try living in the countryside.

Quiet life

Many children had never been to the countryside before. They weren't used to being surrounded by plants and trees, or having so much open space. Some had never seen a cow in real life and were scared of these strange creatures. Lots of villages had only a handful of houses, a post office, a pub and a shop. There was little to do, except make friends with the local children and wander the fields and forests. The chance to explore the countryside was great for the evacuees who had spent most of their lives in cities or towns.

LIKE A HOLIDAY

In the most remote areas of the country, it could feel like the war wasn't happening at all. Every few months, arrangements were made for parents to visit their evacuated children. When they arrived, they would explore the area and catch up on each others' news.

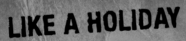

Trying new things

Evacuees who were sent to farming communities often helped their hosts with their daily jobs. The children might bring the cows in from the fields and help with the milking. They also learned how to pluck chickens, make hay bales and skin rabbits. Those in Wales learned another skill – the adults taught them how to speak Welsh and the children introduced them to a few rude words of their own!

Strange games

The countryside offered new ways to have fun, too. Children learned to make whistles from wood and went fishing in the rivers and streams. Each area of the country had its own games, which the evacuees joined in with. One outdoor game, similar to modern hockey, was called 'shinty'. It got its name because the players' shins were hit by the stick as much as the ball was.

Passing the time

Children were kept extremely busy during the war. They were still expected to go to school and help the adults in the evenings and at weekends. However, despite their chores, the children found ways to have fun.

Talking pictures

In the 1940s, there were no computers or mobile phones. Televisions were also rare, but the cinema was a growing attraction – by 1944, half of the country went regularly. Pathé News was shown before each film, providing exciting pictures of the troops in battle, then the main feature would begin. The films of the comic duo Laurel and Hardy were some of the most popular on offer.

The wireless

Almost every house had a wireless radio and it was an important source of information. Special reports described the allied advances in Europe, and which enemy planes had been shot down. The radio also provided shows full of comedy and light entertainment. Children's Hour was a particular favourite. The show included music, wildlife documentaries and plays about the detective Sherlock Holmes. It was broadcast at 5pm, so evacuees could listen to the programme when they got home from school.

DOING THEIR BIT

Many children helped with the war effort. It didn't matter if you were a boy or girl, you helped in any way you could. Children carried messages, helped in the hospitals, watched the skies for planes, and knitted clothes for soldiers on the front line.

War games

The few children left in
the cities roamed the streets,
which were changed dramatically by
the falling bombs. They cycled to the sites of
crashed planes, explored bombsites and searched
ruined houses, finding shrapnel and other souvenirs to
take home. For the poorest children this was the closest they could
get to large, upper-class homes and they enjoyed discovering their
abandoned cellars and the remains of the servants' quarters.

Coming home

By September 1944, World War II was beginning to end. The evacuation process was halted and reversed in all areas except London and the east coast. Londoners had to wait until June 1945 before they were officially allowed to go home.

Some had to stay

It took more than a year for some children to be sent home, and others weren't able to return at all. Millions of houses had been destroyed during the Blitz and some parents had not survived the war. Many of the orphaned children were adopted by their host families. In March 1946, the billeting scheme ended, but 38,000 people were still homeless.

Back home

The children who were able to return had changed since their departure. Some had been away from home for six years and were now young adults, used to a completely different environment. The streets they remembered had changed, too, with churches, shops and houses burned to the ground. Brothers and sisters had been separated and spent hours swapping stories. Some children returned home to hear news of their father's death on the battlefields, and had to get used to another new way of life.

Life changing

All evacuees were deeply affected by their experiences. Some had been moved repeatedly and all of them had been forced to live a different life for years on end. Government reports claimed that the evacuation had gone smoothly, with great benefits for the evacuees and their hosts. They said that it helped different areas of the country to form unbreakable bonds. However, this strongly depended on what life was like for the evacuees while they were away. Some were lucky and left the war with two families and lots of new friends. Others were traumatised by the experience, and just glad to be home.

Some evacuees left their home as children, but returned as adults. Their experiences would stay with them forever.

FOND MEMORIES

As evacuees grew older, it wasn't uncommon for them to go back to the rural areas they had lived in during the war. As adults they remembered the area and wished to return, so they could visit their hosts and the friends they had grown up with.

GLOSSARY

Allotment *A small plot of land set aside for individuals to grow fruit and vegetables.*

Ally *A friendly country, or one that helps another country in times of trouble or war.*

The Armed Forces *The combined power of the British Army, the Royal Air Force and the Royal Navy.*

Armistice *A formal agreement between two opposing armies to stop fighting.*

Billets *Rooms, often in private houses, made temporarily available for soldiers. During World War II, billets were also made available for evacuees.*

Board and lodgings *Food and a place to sleep.*

Civilian *A person not in the Armed Forces.*

The front line *The part of an army that is closest to the enemy.*

Leave *The period of time those serving in the war could spend away from their duties.*

Morale *The feeling in a group. Having good morale means the group is more likely to stick together and survive hard times.*

Pathé News *A UK company that produced news and documentaries from 1910 until 1970.*

Petticoat *An item of clothing worn by women and girls under skirts and dresses.*

Rickets *A condition that causes a child's bones to become soft and weak. The most common cause of rickets is a lack of Vitamin D, found in foods like fish and eggs.*

Spam *Pre-cooked, chopped pork and ham, mixed with salt and water and packaged in a can.*

Further reading

BOOKS

When the Children Came Home by Julie Summers (Simon and Schuster, 2011)

Don't Forget to Write by Pam Hobbs (Ebury Press, 2009)

World War II Sourcebook: Home Front
by Charlie Samuels (Wayland, 2013)

Men, Women and Children in The Second World War
by Peter Hepplewhite (Wayland, 2012)

A Day in the Life of: A World War II Evacuee by Alan Childs (Wayland, 2012)

Goodnight Mr Tom by Michelle Magorian (Puffin, 1981)

WEBSITES

www.nationalarchives.gov.uk/education/world-war-two.htm
This section of The National Archives' website contains lots of information about life in Britain during World War II.

www.bbc.co.uk/schools/primaryhistory/world_war2/
The BBC Learning website about World War II.

www.iwm.org.uk/history/children-during-the-second-world-war
A website from the Imperial War Museum about the lives of children during World War II.

Index